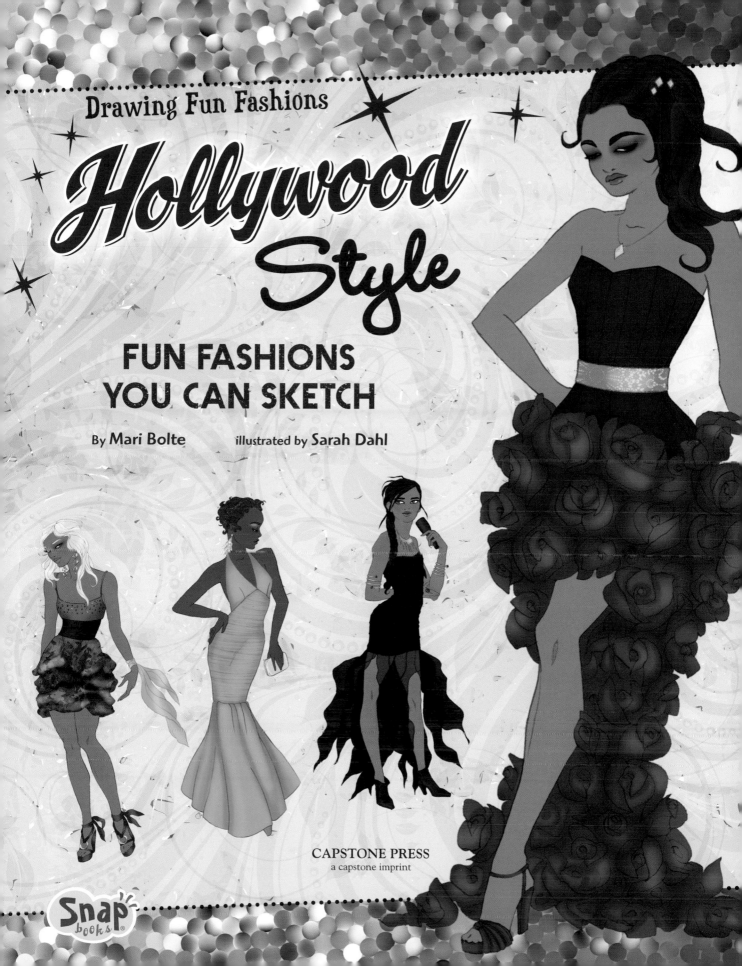

Drawing Fun Fashions

Hollywood Style

FUN FASHIONS YOU CAN SKETCH

By Mari Bolte   illustrated by Sarah Dahl

CAPSTONE PRESS
a capstone imprint

Snap books

Table of Contents

Getting Started

For years, celebrities have walked red carpets and runways in modern, daring dresses. Put pen to paper and recreate these star-powered gowns. Get the look and then twist it to make it your own. Show off your A-list style.

Each outfit shows step-by-step instructions on how to draw your very own fashion model. Build upon simple shapes, and use erasable guidelines to create a human shape.

TIP: Formal dresses come in all sorts of colors and fabrics. Experiment with different art mediums. Watercolors give layered dresses a nice look. Pastels are good for soft, flowy gowns.

STEP 1: Start with a simple line drawing. Pick your favorite pose, and use light guidelines to build your model.

STEP 2: Darken the outlines, and start adding in details like hemlines and hand placements.

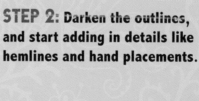

STEP 3: Erase guidelines, and draw in things like fabric prints, hair, facial features, and accessories.

STEP 4: Finish any final details and then add in color, textures, and shading to bring your model to life.

TIP: Experiment with unusual art mediums, such as spray paint, glitter glue, and highlighters.

3

Belle of the Disco Ball

Dance the night away with a flowing chiffon dress. The blending of color creates a unique, one-of-a-kind gown that shines both on and off the dance floor.

TIP: Pastel pencils are the perfect tool to draw this dress's pattern. The tips create distinctive lines of color. Pastels also blend well, giving the dress a soft look.

Short and Sweet

Ring in the new year with noisemakers, fireworks, and a rocking party dress. Your only resolution should be to look this good next year too!

TIP: This dress's simplicity means it's great to experiment with. Give charcoal or graphite pencils a try instead of regular colored pencil or marker.

Red Carpet Ruffles

Catch the camera's attention while walking the red carpet. Shining ruffles will catch the paparazzi's eye and make the front-page news.

TIP: A metallic marker or white graphite pencil will help the dress shine.

Outshine any award with a dress as fluid as liquid metal. Nothing goes with a gold statue like a molten metal dress.

TIP: Use watercolors to color the dress. Sprinkle salt onto wet watercolor wherever you want to add shine. Once the paint has dried, carefully brush the salt off. The salt will create the textured effect on the dress.

STAR-STUDDED SHEATH

A sheath dress flatters most body types. This style also adds a touch of old-fashioned elegance to any formal event. While no necklace is needed, chandelier earrings bring just the right touch of glam.

TIP: Sheath dresses look good with many kinds of necklines. V-neck, halter, strapless, plunging, one-shoulder, and sleeved tops all work with a sheath dress.

21st Century Princess

A modern princess doesn't need Prince Charming to escort her anywhere. Whether on the way to a movie premiere or stopping off at the prom, the Hollywood princess is her own hero.

TIP: Study classic movie princess gowns and combine them with modern trends. You'll come up with something timeless and worthy of red-carpet royalty.

Floral Formal

Who needs a corsage when you've brought your own bouquet? Roses are seen as a symbol of love and beauty, and so should you.

TIP: Use more than one art medium to create the two different hues of red. Color the top of the dress with marker. Draw the roses with watercolors or watercolor pencils.

17

Hollywood Glam

Hollywood style isn't just about being girly. Show the world that dresses can be bold with uneven lines and deep colors. Add a touch of rock star with fringe and feathers.

TIP: Don't overthink the dress's ruffles. Draw them once and stick with them. They're meant to be free-flowing and loose.

Hall of Famer

TIP: Stick to single colors for the accessories. The dress is colorful enough on its own.

A rocker in the hall of fame has reached the height of stardom! Dress like you're at the top even if you're still on the waiting list. This outfit will dazzle any crowd.

Glitz and Gauze

Dressing up can make you feel like you're walking on air. Add a glitzy haze to your outfit with layers of soft chiffon. Then light the way with crystals and a few sparkling jewels.

TIP: To make this outfit really pop, glue small rhinestones to the dress. A toothpick or jewelry picker is a great tool to place gems.

BackStage GLAM

Presenters and musical acts are essential to the success of any awards show. Have the audience cheering for an encore with this fabulous dress.

TIP: Use a thin-tipped black, blue, or silver permanent marker to outline the dress's layers.

Think Pink

Being a starlet is all about youth and energy. Act your age in a short sweetheart dress with a ruffled hemline. A contrasting chiffon scarf catches the eye and adds a pop of color.

TIP: Use watercolors for the dress. While the paint is wet, add color to the skirt. Once the paint is dry, paint the jewels onto the bodice.

27

TIP: If you find you like Asian-inspired dresses, add them to your sketchbook. Use Asian prints to put a twist on the ordinary prom dress.

ASIAN INSPIRED

Dress designs and prints from around the world freshen up the formal scene. Traditional Japanese clothing lends itself to bright colors and modern prints. Updated accessories, such as hair ornaments and umbrellas, are tickets to the international stage.

Extra Accessories

Use your creativity to create original accessories for each outfit. Each piece will reflect your personal style and taste! Take your time and figure out what works for you. Don't forget that accessories complete the outfit.

TIP: Formal trends come and go, but stylists aren't afraid to look to the past. Be fearless! Plaids, animal prints, costume jewelry, and hats are just a few ideas for the vintage-inspired formal line.

Read More

Hibbert, Clare. *Movie Star.* Celeb. Mankato, Minn.: Sea-to-Sea Publications, 2012.

Thomas, Isabel. *Being a Fashion Stylist.* Awesome Jobs. Minneapolis: Lerner Publications Co., 2013.

Wooster, Patricia. *Fashion Designer.* Cool Arts Careers. Ann Arbor, Mich.: Cherry Lake Pub., 2012.

Internet Sites

FactHound offers a safe, fun way to find Internet sites related to this book. All of the sites on FactHound have been researched by our staff.

Here's all you do:

Visit *www.facthound.com*

Type in this code: 9781620650370

Super-cool stuff! Check out projects, games and lots more at **www.capstonekids.com**

Snap Books are published by Capstone Press,
1710 Roe Crest Drive, North Mankato, Minnesota 56003
www.capstonepub.com

Copyright © 2013 by Capstone Press, a Capstone imprint. All rights reserved. No part of this publication may be reproduced in whole or in part, or stored in a retrieval system, or transmitted in any formor by any means, electronic, mechanical, photocopying, recording, or otherwise, without written permission of the publisher.

Library of Congress Cataloging-in-Publication Data
Bolte, Mari.
  Hollywood style : fun fashions you can sketch / by Mari Bolte.
    pages cm — (Snap. Drawing fun fashions)
  Summary: "Lively text and fun illustrations describe how to draw cool fashions"—Provided by publisher.
  ISBN 978-1-62065-037-0 (library binding)
  ISBN 978-1-4765-1776-6 (ebook PDF)
1. Fashion drawing—Juvenile literature. I. Title.

  TT509.B653 2013
  741.6'72—dc23   2012028399

Editorial Credits
Lori Bye and Ashlee Suker, designers; Nathan Gassman, art director; Marcie Spence, media researcher;
    Laura Manthe, production specialist

The illustrations in this book were created digitally.
Design elements by Shutterstock.

Printed in the United States of America in North Mankato, Minnesota.
092012   006933CGS13